## KATE SUMMERSCALE

Kate Summerscale is the author of the number-one bestselling *The Suspicions of Mr Whicher*, published in 2008, winner of the Samuel Johnson Prize for Non-Fiction and the Galaxy British Book of the Year Award. Her debut, *The Queen of Whale Cay*, won a Somerset Maugham Award and was shortlisted for the Whitbread Biography Award. *The Wicked Boy*, published in 2016, won the Mystery Writers of America Edgar Award for Best Fact Crime, and *The Haunting of Alma Fielding*, published in 2020, was shortlisted for the Baillie Gifford Prize for Non-Fiction. Her latest publication is *The Book of Phobias and Manias: A History of the World in 99 Obsessions*. She lives in north London.

## ALEXANDRA WOOD

Plays include *The Tyler Sisters* and *The Empty Quarter* (Hampstead); co-writer of *Silence*, an adaptation of Kavita Puri's *Partition Voices* (Donmar Warehouse/Tara Theatre); *Descent* (Audible Originals); *Never Vera Blue* (Futures Theatre); *The Initiate* and *The Human Ear* (Paines Plough); *Ages* (Old Vic New Voices); a translation of Manfred Karge's *Man to Man* (Wales Millennium Centre); *Merit* (Plymouth Drum); an adaptation of Jung Chang's *Wild Swans* (Young Vic/ART); *Twelve Years* (Radio 4); *Unbroken* (Gate) and *The Eleventh Capital* (Royal Court).

Short plays include *Ariadne on the Beach* (Unicorn Theatre); *Invitation Interrupted* (Donmar Warehouse); *The Driving Rage* and *Pope's Grotto* (Paines Plough); *My Name is Tania Head* (part of *Decade*, Headlong).

Alexandra is a past winner of the George Devine Award and has been Playwright-in-Residence at Paines Plough.

**Other Titles in This Series**

1984
Nick Hern
*Adapted from* George Orwell

AROUND THE WORLD IN 80 DAYS
Laura Eason
*Adapted from* Jules Verne

BLEAK EXPECTATIONS
Mark Evans

A CHRISTMAS CAROL
David Edgar
*Adapted from* Charles Dickens

A CHRISTMAS CAROL – A GHOST
 STORY
Mark Gatiss
*Adapted from* Charles Dickens

A CHRISTMAS CAROL: A FAIRY TALE
Piers Torday
*Adapted from* Charles Dickens

CORAM BOY
Helen Edmundson
*Adapted from* Jamila Gavin

DAVID COPPERFIELD
Alastair Cording
*Adapted from* Charles Dickens

DIARY OF A NOBODY
Hugh Osborne
*Adapted from* George & Weedon Grossmith

DRACULA: THE BLOODY TRUTH
Le Navet Bete & John Nicholson
*Adapted from* Bram Stoker

EMMA
Martin Millar and Doon MacKichan
*Adapted from* Jane Austen

THE GOOD LIFE
Jeremy Sams
*Adapted from* John Esmonde
 and Bob Larbey

GREAT EXPECTATIONS
Jo Clifford
*Adapted from* Charles Dickens

GREAT EXPECTATIONS
Nick Ormerod and Declan Donnellan
*Adapted from* Charles Dickens

THE HAUNTING
Hugh Janes
*Adapted from* Charles Dickens

THE HOUND OF THE BASKERVILLES
Steven Canny & John Nicholson
*Adapted from* Arthur Conan Doyle

JANE EYRE
Chris Bush
*Adapted from* Charlotte Brontë

JEEVES AND WOOSTER IN
 'PERFECT NONSENSE'
The Goodale Brothers
*Adapted from* P.G. Wodehouse

JEKYLL AND HYDE
Neil Bartlett
*Adapted from* Robert Louis Stevenson

LITTLE WOMEN
Anne-Marie Casey
*Adapted from* Louisa May Alcott

THE MASSIVE TRAGEDY OF
 MADAME BOVARY
John Nicholson & Javier Marzan
*Adapted from* Gustave Flaubert

MY FAMILY AND OTHER ANIMALS
Janys Chambers
*Adapted from* Gerald Durrell

NORTHANGER ABBEY
Tim Luscombe
*Adapted from* Jane Austen

NOUGHTS & CROSSES
Dominic Cooke
*Adapted from* Malorie Blackman

ORLANDO
Neil Bartlett
*Adapted from* Virginia Woolf

PERSUASION
Mark Healy
*Adapted from* Jane Austen

PRIDE AND PREJUDICE* (*SORT OF)
Isobel McArthur
*Adapted from* Jane Austen

THE RAILWAY CHILDREN
Mike Kenny
*Adapted from* E. Nesbit

SWALLOWS AND AMAZONS
Helen Edmundson and Neil Hannon
*Adapted from* Arthur Ransome

A TALE OF TWO CITIES
Mike Poulton
*Adapted from* Charles Dickens

THE TAXIDERMIST'S DAUGHTER
Kate Mosse

THE THREE MUSKETEERS
John Nicholson & Le Navet Bete
*Adapted from* Alexander Dumas

TREASURE ISLAND
John Nicholson & Le Navet Bete
*Adapted from* Robert Louis Stevenson

WENDY & PETER PAN
Ella Hickson
*Adapted from* J. M. Barrie

Kate Summerscale

# THE SUSPICIONS OF MR WHICHER

*Adapted for the stage by*
Alexandra Wood

## NICK HERN BOOKS

London

www.nickhernbooks.co.uk

**A Nick Hern Book**

This adaptation of *The Suspicions of Mr Whicher* first published in Great Britain as a paperback original in 2023 by Nick Hern Books Limited, The Glasshouse, 49a Goldhawk Road, London W12 8QP

*The Suspicions of Mr Whicher* (book) copyright © 2008 Kate Summerscale
*The Suspicions of Mr Whicher* (play) copyright © 2023 Alexandra Wood

Alexandra Wood has asserted her right to be identified as the author of this adaptation

Cover design by Rebecca Pitt Creative

Designed and typeset by Nick Hern Books, London
Printed in Great Britain by Mimeo Ltd, Huntingdon, Cambridgeshire PE29 6XX

A CIP catalogue record for this book is available from the British Library

ISBN 978 1 83904 240 9

This adaptation of *The Suspicions of Mr Whicher* was first performed at the Watermill Theatre, Newbury, on 5 May 2023. The cast was as follows:

MR KENT *and Others* — Jim Creighton
JONATHAN WHICHER — Christopher Naylor
WILLIAM *and Others* — Sam Liu
MISS GOUGH *and Others* — Robyn Sinclair
MRS KENT (NÉE MISS PRATT) *and Others* — Connie Walker
CONSTANCE KENT — Eleanor Wyld
BOY / DENIS — Hector Philpott
Clara Tame
Samuel Wall

*Director* — Kate Budgen
*Designer* — Amy Jane Cook
*Lighting Designer* — Katy Morison
*Sound Designer and Composer* — Beth Duke
*Video Projection Designer* — Rachel Sampley
*Movement and Intimacy Director* — Angela Gasparetto
*Production Manager* — Nick Flintoff
*Assistant Production Manager* — Alice Reddick
*Costume Supervisor* — Emily Barratt
*Deputy Costume Supervisor* — Beth Rose
*Costume Maker* — Ros Kitson
*Company Stage Manager* — Cat Pewsey
*Deputy Stage Manager* — Emily Stedman
*Assistant Stage Manager* — Natalie Toney
*Placement Assistant Stage Manager* — Phoebe Butcher
*Head of Technical* — Thom Townsend
*Theatre Technician* — Izzy Moore
*Production Electricians* — Keith Anker
Ryan Tate
*Audio Description* — Lixi Chivas
*Set Construction* — DSH Carpentry

## Characters

JONATHAN WHICHER, *forty-five to sixty-six*
CONSTANCE KENT, *five to thirty-six*
MISS PRATT, *twenty-eight, who becomes*
    MRS KENT, *thirty-six to forty*
MR KENT, *forty-seven to sixty-four*
JOHN FOLEY, *sixty-four*
ELIZABETH GOUGH, *twenty-two*
WILLIAM KENT, *eleven to eighteen*
EDWARD KENT, *eighteen*
DR PARSONS, *forty-five*
LOUISA HATHERILL, *fifteen*
SARAH COX, *twenty-two*
PETER EDLIN, *forty*
GUARD
BOY, *three*
CROWD
DENIS, *four*
REVEREND WAGNER
KATHARINE GREAM
PASSENGER
SIR THOMAS HENRY
EMILIE, *fifty-one*
OLDER WILLIAM, *fifty*
NURSE
ARTHUR

**Notes on the Text**

Whicher and Constance should be played by the same two
performers throughout. The other parts may be played by
members of an ensemble.

The scenes should flow into one another. Constance and
Whicher remain in Fulham Prison, even when they recall scenes
from the past.

The sections in **bold** are Constance's memories, distinct from
memories of the investigation and trial. Whicher doesn't
experience these.

A forward slash ( / ) indicates a point of interruption.

A lack of punctuation at the end of a line indicates that the
character cannot, or does not wish to, continue.

A line space in between sections indicates a shift in time.

*This text went to press before the end of rehearsals and so may
differ slightly from the play as performed.*

## ACT ONE

*Fulham Prison, early 1881.* WHICHER *is sixty-six,*
CONSTANCE *is thirty-six.*

WHICHER. You've applied for early release three times.

CONSTANCE. I intend to apply again.

WHICHER. You believe you should be free?

CONSTANCE. I don't believe I'm a threat.

Reverend Wagner has written on my behalf. Others have,
too. They moved me here from Millbank, which was a small
concession, I suppose.

WHICHER. You murdered your three-year-old brother.

CONSTANCE. I'll never forgive myself.

But I believe I could do some good, be of some use to society
now.

WHICHER. I moved to Battersea last year but before that I
lived just beyond the walls of Millbank Prison.

I thought of you in there.

CONSTANCE. Do you often think about past cases?

*Pause.*

WHICHER. This case haunts me.

I don't doubt your guilt, but it's not the full truth, is it?

I don't want to die without knowing that.

CONSTANCE. Are you dying?

WHICHER. I'm not in my prime.

*Pause.*

I've spent most of my life pursuing the Truth and it's often felt like a game. I've prided myself on being able to read people, on sparring and outsmarting them, and on knowing, on knowing I'm right, on certainty, on offering people an answer and on the comfort that brings.

Certainty.

But I don't have that here, and it makes me question whether it's even possible, or whether I spent my life in pursuit of an illusion, in fact, whether I've wasted my time, whether I've wasted my time on this earth.

CONSTANCE. I've spent sixteen years in prison. My youth. I know about wasted time.

*Pause.*

WHICHER. I could help you.

CONSTANCE. How?

WHICHER. I could write a letter in support of your early release, like Reverend Wagner.

CONSTANCE. Why would you do that?

WHICHER. If you tell me the full truth of what happened. Just me. Just for my own

*Pause.*

Do you have many visitors?

*Pause.*

CONSTANCE. I don't know what else I can tell you.

WHICHER. If we're thorough, if we go through it all / with absolute

CONSTANCE. Again?

WHICHER. One last time. If we tread carefully, pay attention to the details, if we are meticulous and uncompromising, / that missing

CONSTANCE. You were all those things before.

WHICHER. that missing piece, that fullness, must be revealed.

CONSTANCE. And what if it isn't?

WHICHER. I believe it will be.

CONSTANCE. How much is a letter from you worth now, Mr Whicher? It's a long time since you've been considered the prince of detectives.

WHICHER. You've had three failed attempts, isn't it worth a try?

CONSTANCE. I've been through it all too many times.

WHICHER. Might not a letter from the detective responsible for your case carry some weight?

You're right, I don't have the influence I once had. But without some new advocacy in your next appeal, how much hope can you really have?

*A clap of thunder. The sounds of a storm.*

*The library.* **MISS PRATT** (*twenty-eight*) *rushes onto the stage towards* **MR KENT** (*forty-seven*)*, who pulls her down onto his knee and kisses her. She sees* **CONSTANCE.**

**MISS PRATT. Not before the child!**

**MR KENT. It's only human nature, Mary**.

*He kisses her again and she responds.*

CONSTANCE. Where would you want to begin?

WHICHER. Monday the sixteenth of July, 1860.

CONSTANCE. Saville was already dead by then.

WHICHER. A full two weeks after the murder. But it's only then that the local constabulary request assistance from the Metropolitan detective force.

Superintendent Foley shows me the drawing room.

FOLEY. The housemaid found the door unlocked and this window slightly open. The shutters are fastened with that bar, no one could have come in from outside, so as horrifying as it is, the murder must've been committed by someone in the house.

WHICHER. That's eleven people?

FOLEY. Yes, but four of those are children, who wouldn't be capable.

WHICHER. William is fifteen, Constance sixteen. I frequently come across children as young as eight capable of theft and deceit.

FOLEY. But murder?

WHICHER. In certain circumstances.

FOLEY. Perhaps where you're from, detective, children are more disturbed.

In my opinion, the number of people within the house capable of carrying out such a murder is no more than six.

WHICHER. And who are they, in your opinion?

FOLEY. Samuel Kent, the boy's father.

Mary Ann and Elizabeth, the two eldest daughters from his first marriage, although I highly doubt either of them have it in them.

Miss Gough, the nursemaid.

Miss Cox, the housemaid.

And Miss Kerslake, the cook.

WHICHER. And Mrs Kent?

FOLEY. She's eight months pregnant. She could barely lift the boy, let alone carry him from the nursery, down the stairs, through the window, to the privy. And besides the practical impossibility, she was his devoted mother.

WHICHER. I've dealt with more than one case of a mother murdering her child, but at such a late stage of pregnancy, it does seem unlikely she could manage it alone.

It's possible the window wasn't used in the crime at all. Perhaps the murderer only opened the window so we'd think the child had been stolen away across the fields.

FOLEY. That doesn't help us, does it? Since the child was in fact stabbed and thrown into the privy.

WHICHER. It could offer us a glimpse into the murderer's state of mind though. If it was meant to deceive us, it suggests he or she

FOLEY. Or they.

WHICHER. were relatively calm. That perhaps this had been planned for some time. Years in the making, who knows.

**CONSTANCE***'s attention is drawn again to the library.*

**MR KENT. It's only human nature, Mary.**

*He kisses* **MISS PRATT** *again and she responds. The thunder sounds and they stop.*

**MISS PRATT. Come here, Constance, are you scared of the storm?**

**CONSTANCE** *goes over to them.*

**MR KENT. There's nothing to be scared of, it's only thunder.**

*She stares at them.*

**Why are you looking at me like that?**

**MISS PRATT. She's a good girl, aren't you, Constance? Not like that crazy mother of yours.**

**MR KENT** (*to* **MISS PRATT**). **She's lucky to have you.**

WHICHER. Was it years in the making?

**MISS PRATT (*to* CONSTANCE). We're lucky to have each other, aren't we?**

WHICHER. Constance?

CONSTANCE. This won't help.

WHICHER. There are things I've missed, they're there I just haven't seen them yet.

CONSTANCE. No good can come from this.

WHICHER. Don't you want to be free?

CONSTANCE. Free of this, this story, as much as these walls, and going over it all again / isn't going to

WHICHER. It's not a story.

CONSTANCE. It's become one.

WHICHER. No. These things happened.

CONSTANCE. Yes, they happened, but other things can happen, too, Mr Whicher. I can do good, but when all anyone asks me about is something I did over twenty years / ago

WHICHER. Do people ask?

Does anyone really ask any more, Constance?

CONSTANCE. You're asking me.

WHICHER. We might be the only two people in the world who still think about this crime.

CONSTANCE. None of my family will ever forget what happened to Saville.

WHICHER. Does it haunt them like it haunts you?

I want to be free of this crime as much as you do.

CONSTANCE *laughs*.

Are you laughing at me?

CONSTANCE. You're asking me to free you. Me.

WHICHER. I think you can. If you choose to. Will you help me?

*Pause.*

*She makes a small gesture to indicate they may continue with their recollections.*

I interviewed the nursemaid, Miss Gough.


WHICHER. Was Saville a heavy sleeper, Miss Gough?

GOUGH. Yes.

WHICHER. And yourself?

GOUGH. I slept heavily too, it'd been an arduous day.

WHICHER. Can you describe for me what you did on the evening of Friday the twenty-ninth of June?

GOUGH. At seven-thirty I put Eveline in her cot, next to my bed in the nursery. Then I went downstairs and gave Saville a laxative. Mrs Kent was there, it'd been prescribed by the doctor.

At eight o'clock I put him in his cot in the nursery and I put Mary Amelia in her bed, she sleeps in her parents' room.

I ate my supper and joined everyone else for evening prayers. Then I / went back up to


WHICHER. What did you pray for that night?

CONSTANCE. I don't think I prayed at all. Not like I do now.

I was probably going over what I was about to do.

WHICHER. You didn't pray for forgiveness?

*The family group pray together on the evening of 29th June
1860.*

**MR KENT. Father, whose nature and property is ever to
have mercy and to forgive, receive our humble petitions;
and though we be tied and bound with the chain of our
sins, yet let the pitifulness of thy great mercy loose us**

GOUGH. When I went back to the nursery, Saville was lying as
he usually did, with his face to the wall and his arm under his
head. Mrs Kent came to kiss the children goodnight. I tucked
the bedclothes around him, bolted the windows and went to
sleep.

WHICHER. What time did you wake on Saturday the thirtieth?

GOUGH. Five o'clock.

WHICHER. And did you notice anything unusual?

GOUGH. Saville wasn't in his cot, but the bed clothes were
put back neatly, so I assumed his mother had heard him
crying and taken him to her own room, but when I knocked
at Mr and Mrs Kent's room and asked if the children were
awake, she said what do you mean by children, there's
only one child, she meant Mary Amelia who sleeps in their
room. I asked if Master Saville wasn't with her, and she said
certainly not. I said he wasn't in the nursery, and she asked
why I hadn't roused her immediately, and I told her I thought
he was with you.

WHICHER. Even though she would've struggled to carry him
in her current condition?

GOUGH. I feel terrible for not raising the alarm earlier, but the
truth is, it still would've been too late.

WHICHER. How did the rest of the family respond to the news
of his disappearance?

GOUGH. I went to ask Mary Ann and Elizabeth if they'd seen him, but they hadn't. Miss Constance came out from her room, which is next to theirs, but she didn't make any comment.

WHICHER. And Master William?

GOUGH. His room is further along the landing, so he may not have heard us.

WHICHER. When the police searcher was examining you, Miss Gough, you told her this was done through jealousy.

CONSTANCE. Not jealousy.

WHICHER. The little boy goes into his mamma's room and tells everything, you said.

What did you mean by that?

GOUGH. I was trying to understand.

WHICHER. It sounds as if you had a specific incident in mind.

GOUGH *shakes her head*.

Was Saville a tell-tale?

GOUGH. No more than any three-year-old.

WHICHER. Do you have a lover?

GOUGH. I'm not accustomed to such questions.

WHICHER. Did Saville wake and see you with a lover?

GOUGH. I don't have a

WHICHER. Did you kill Saville before he could tell more tales?

GOUGH. No.

*A knock at a door. The door opens.*

**MR KENT** *enters the room.* **MISS PRATT** *is waiting. The child Constance is asleep in the room.*

**MISS PRATT.** Quietly, Samuel.

**MR KENT** (*half-whispering*). That girl would sleep through Armageddon.

*He goes to* **MISS PRATT** *and they embrace.*

**MISS PRATT.** I hate this secrecy.

**MR KENT.** It's a little fun too, isn't it?

**MISS PRATT.** Why should you have to put up with that lunatic?

**MR KENT.** She's my wife.

**MISS PRATT.** She belongs in an asylum.

**MR KENT** (*laughing*). Shhh.

**MISS PRATT.** A cage.

**MR KENT.** Just as well I have you to comfort me.

**MISS PRATT.** And what can I do to comfort you this evening, Mr Kent?

*A noise from the other side of the room, the child Constance is stirring.*

*They look in her direction.*

**She's asleep.**

CONSTANCE. Miss Gough was a heavy sleeper. She never even stirred when I went into the nursery that night.

I've always been a light sleeper.

WHICHER. A troubled conscience perhaps.

CONSTANCE. Not when I was a small girl.

   Things happened that I couldn't understand. I never wanted
   to miss something that might help me.

WHICHER. Did William help you understand?

CONSTANCE. He helped me survive. We helped each other.


WHICHER. I would like to speak to you alone, Miss Kent.

CONSTANCE. There's nothing I'm ashamed to talk about in
   front of my brother.

WILLIAM. I won't say anything.

CONSTANCE. We share everything anyway.

WHICHER. You returned from school on the fifteenth of June.

CONSTANCE. Yes.

WHICHER (*holds up a list*). This is the list of linen you brought
   back with you. It says you returned with three nightdresses.
   I searched your room and I can only find two. What
   happened to the other one?

CONSTANCE. It was lost at the wash.

WHICHER. Do you know how long Mrs Holley has been doing
   the laundry for your family?

CONSTANCE. Since we moved here, probably.

WHICHER. And do you know how many items have gone
   missing in that time?

CONSTANCE. Nothing of mine before.

WHICHER. Just two items in five years. An old duster and an
   old towel.

   It seems very unlucky that your nightdress should go missing
   at such a critical moment.

CONSTANCE. Maybe I am unlucky.

WHICHER. I find that hard to believe.

CONSTANCE. Why? Because of my fine surroundings?


WHICHER. Do you think you're unlucky?

CONSTANCE. No more than any of the other women in here.

WHICHER. Did you, at the time?

CONSTANCE. Nothing excuses what I did.


WHICHER. Why might someone want a nightdress to go
    missing?

CONSTANCE. I don't know.

WHICHER. If it was stained, perhaps, in a way that suggested
    they'd been involved in the murder.

    WILLIAM *shifts, drawing* WHICHER*'s attention.*

CONSTANCE. But my nightdress wasn't stained. Miss Cox and
    my sisters saw it when they packed the laundry basket.

WHICHER. Mrs Holley says it wasn't in the laundry basket.

CONSTANCE. Perhaps she was distracted. She knew my
    brother, we've all been affected.

WHICHER. This is a very difficult time for your family.

CONSTANCE. One of them.

WHICHER. Have there been many?

CONSTANCE. Perhaps no more than average, it's hard to know
    what goes on in other families. But I suppose that's your job.


CONSTANCE. Do you have a family?

    You know so much about mine, and even that's not enough.
    I know nothing of yours.

WHICHER. I have a wife.

CONSTANCE. What's her name?

WHICHER. Charlotte.

CONSTANCE. Do you love her?

*Pause.*

Sorry, is that a difficult question?

WHICHER. I do.

CONSTANCE. Children?

WHICHER. We looked after two girls.

CONSTANCE. Did you have any of your own?

*Silence.*

It's not easy to go back over the past, is it.

You said you want to be free of this crime as much as I do. Don't you think it's outrageous to compare your experience to mine?

WHICHER. This case changed the course of my life. After this I never, I lost

CONSTANCE. Lost what?

What did you really lose?

*Pause.*

Do you think you've lived vicariously, Mr Whicher?

All that time spent interrogating other people's desires, their wrongdoings, examining other people's lives and never really living your own.

WHICHER. You're doing the same thing now as you did then. When I asked about your missing nightdress, you diverted attention. I knew the nightdress was the key, the missing piece, but two weeks after the crime, I never had a chance of finding it, did I?

CONSTANCE. Our eldest brother, Edward, was in the Merchant Navy. We thought he was drowned once, but he came back from the dead. He died for real in Havana a few years later though. He couldn't stand to be here either.

WHICHER. Are Edward's adventures what inspired you and William four years ago?

CONSTANCE. We only got as far as Bath.

WHICHER. But you were heading for the sea?

CONSTANCE. We were going to be cabin boys.

WHICHER. Both of you?

CONSTANCE. Why not?

WHICHER. So you cut your hair and wore your brother's old clothes?

CONSTANCE. Yes.

WHICHER. And where did you discard your hair and your clothes?

CONSTANCE. Down the same place where my little brother was found.

WHICHER. Whose idea was that?

CONSTANCE. Mine.

WHICHER. And once you'd done that, you and William set off for Bristol.

CONSTANCE. Yes, but the innkeeper at Bath suspected we were runaways and raised the alarm.

WHICHER. Whose idea was it?

CONSTANCE. I persuaded William to go with me.

WILLIAM. I wanted to go.

CONSTANCE. I persuaded him.

WHICHER. You're very close.

CONSTANCE. He's my favourite of my brothers and sisters. We write to each other when we're at school.

WHICHER. Were you fond of Saville?

CONSTANCE. Very. But he used not to be fond of me.

WHICHER. Why do you think that was?

CONSTANCE. Perhaps because I teased him. But he seemed fonder of me these holidays.

WHICHER. I spoke to your school friend, Emma Moody, who told me you disliked Saville and pinched him.

CONSTANCE. It was said in jest, I never struck or pinched him.

WHICHER. Why did you tease him?

CONSTANCE. Isn't that what older siblings do?

WHICHER. Miss Moody believes it was through jealousy, because your parents showed great partiality to the younger children, do you agree with that?

CONSTANCE. I'm not jealous, no.

WHICHER. Is it true that your father's second family are much better treated than his first?

CONSTANCE. I have never been mistreated.


WHICHER. Do you still think that?


**MR KENT** (*laughing*). **Shhh.**

**MISS PRATT. A cage.**

**MR KENT. Just as well I have you to comfort me.**

**MISS PRATT. And what can I do to comfort you this evening, Mr Kent?**

CONSTANCE. My mother was mistreated.

**CONSTANCE** *overhears her older brother* **EDWARD**
(*eighteen*) *and* **MR KENT** (*fifty-two*).

**EDWARD. Have you no shame, Father?**

**MR KENT. What do I have to be ashamed about?**

**EDWARD. Your children's governess.**

**MR KENT. She'll be an excellent mother.**

**EDWARD. You're all but announcing the rumours were
    true. The government inspector, his wife and the
    governess.**

**MR KENT. Your mother is dead, I'm a free man.**

**EDWARD. And what do you think killed her?**

**MR KENT. An obstruction of the bowel.**

**EDWARD. You don't think it killed her to have to live in
    this house with you and her carrying on so brazenly? The
    servants knew it, everyone did, that's why we've had to
    move so often.**

**MR KENT. There are other rumours too, Edward.**

    **Are you upset by my marriage for your mother or for
    yourself?**

**EDWARD. I'd want nothing to do with a woman like Mary
    Pratt.**

**MR KENT. Not now, maybe.**

**EDWARD. You disgust me.**

    *The sound of* **CONSTANCE** *moving.*

**MR KENT. Who's there?**

CONSTANCE. My mother wasn't mad. They poisoned me against her.

WHICHER. Your father appeared to me to be a decent man. Sentimental, even. He appeared to feel genuine affection for his children.

CONSTANCE. He also took any opportunity to satisfy his own desires, like those he felt for the woman who became my stepmother.

MR KENT. I'll answer what I can but my mind has been unsteady since it happened.

WHICHER. When it was first discovered Saville was missing, what did you do, Mr Kent?

MR KENT. I sent for the local constables, then I rode to Trowbridge to fetch Superintendent Foley.

WHICHER. Why did you choose to ride there yourself, when someone else could have sent a message?

MR KENT. I was in a phaeton, no officer could've made the journey faster.

WHICHER. It would've given you an opportunity to dispose of incriminating evidence.

MR KENT. I wanted to ensure the message got through, that was the sole reason. I wanted to send for a London detective right there and then, I was fearful traces of the crime would disappear or be destroyed. Foley worried about intruding on my family's privacy but I told him he mustn't feel under the slightest restraint.

WHICHER. From everything I've heard, Saville was a playful, good-tempered boy, a general favourite.

MR KENT. He would've made a fine man.

WHICHER. Was he similar to his brother William?

MR KENT. No, they were nothing alike, William's a timid boy.

*July 1856.* **WILLIAM** (*eleven*) *holds scissors to* **CONSTANCE**'*s* (*twelve*) *head.*

**WILLIAM. Are you sure?**

**CONSTANCE. Do it.**

*He cuts off her hair. She squeals in delight.*

**WILLIAM. We'll be brothers!**

*She takes off her dress and petticoats.*

**Here, give them to me, I'll throw them down the privy, no one will look there.**

**WILLIAM** *gathers up the dress and cut hair.*

**Meet me by the gate.**

**WILLIAM** *exits and* **CONSTANCE** *puts on his old clothes.*


WHICHER. What do you make of the rumours William committed the murder?

MR KENT. There have been endless rumours. I think all but one-year-old Eveline have been suspected at some point.

WHICHER. But do you think him capable?

MR KENT. I don't make a habit of accusing my children of the most abhorrent crime imaginable. I have my reasons for thinking Constance responsible.

WHICHER. The two of them are very close.

MR KENT. Yes, but she's an independent girl. Prides herself on it. I don't think she'd need assistance.

My first wife underwent a bout of insanity while she was pregnant with Constance, which makes her more liable to go mad herself.

CONSTANCE. My mother wasn't mad. My siblings used to stay in her wing of the house. Even William. I was the only one who would stay with my father and the woman I was told to call Mamma. They poisoned me against my own mother.

MR KENT. Most madness is hereditary, the mother is the strongest source and the daughter the most likely recipient. I am a mere government inspector, I don't claim to understand such things fully, but physicians I know inform me this is the case.

CONSTANCE. I am not mad, and I did not need, or want, to use that as a defence.

MR KENT. I've been plagued by a memory of something that happened last year. Minor at the time, but now it feels more significant.

Saville had been put to bed in a pair of knitted socks. But the next morning the nursemaid found they had been removed. The socks were found later, one on the nursery table, the other in Mrs Kent's bedroom.

WHICHER. Why has it been plaguing you?

MR KENT. There's a gentleness required, removing a sleeping child's socks, without waking him. Not gentle maybe, but careful, controlled. Was it a rehearsal for the murder?

My wife and Constance were the only ones who could've been responsible. I was away on business and my eldest daughters were on a visit.

WHICHER. Was it a rehearsal?

**CONSTANCE** (*five*) *sits with* **MISS PRATT**.

**CONSTANCE. Mother said she'd like to see more of me and I said, can't you see all of me? Have you got a problem with your eyes, along with all your other problems, I said, and she went quiet, and so I said, have you got a problem with your ears, too, and she didn't say anything, so I said, have you got a problem with your tongue as well and she stayed quiet, so I said, and you wonder why I prefer my other Mamma?**

**MISS PRATT** *smiles*.


MR KENT. I was watching Eveline sleep last night, and I couldn't imagine doing something that might mean her feet were cold, let alone

what was done to Saville.

Under my roof.

A father's most basic duty is to keep his children safe. As I watched Eveline sleep I was overcome with fear that the same would happen to her.

Please don't think I find it easy to imagine Constance capable of such evil, let alone voice it to you, but it is my duty to keep my family safe.


CONSTANCE. His duty to my mother never concerned him.

WHICHER. What was done to Saville, that's the thing I

Even if I can understand your reasons for wanting revenge, it only takes me so far. Then I come up against the reality of what you did.

CONSTANCE. I'll never forgive myself.

WHICHER. When I spoke to Doctor Parsons about his post-mortem, I was

the savagery.

PARSONS. I estimated he must've been killed before three o'clock that morning. The throat was cut to the bone by a sharp instrument, from left to right.

CONSTANCE. We both know what was done.

PARSONS. There was also a stab to the chest, which had cut through the clothes and the cartilage of two ribs.

WHICHER. Which of these injuries do you think killed him?

PARSONS. Neither. I believe he was suffocated, at least partly, before he was then attacked with a knife.

I knew Mr Dickens while I lived in London, something tells me he'll be intrigued by this case.

WHICHER. Why do you think he was suffocated?

PARSONS. It would account for the darkness around his lips, and the lack of blood on the privy walls. His heart had been stilled before the wound was inflicted, so his blood didn't burst out.

Do you know Mr Dickens's work?

WHICHER. If Saville was suffocated, as you suggest, perhaps he was killed impulsively to secure his silence. If he'd witnessed Miss Gough and Mr Kent in bed together, for example.

PARSONS. Mr Kent is an inspector of factories.

WHICHER. Yes.

PARSONS. As such, he is generally disliked in this district. He's an agent of surveillance, as you are, and nobody likes those.

Local law enforcement are happy to believe Samuel Kent was having an illicit affair with the nursemaid and that he killed his son to cover it up, but there's no doubt in my mind that Constance is the killer. When I examined her nightdress that Saturday, not only was it free of any incriminating stains, it was remarkably clean, in fact I would say it was a fresh nightgown, not one that had been worn six days.

WHICHER. I need more than an anecdote about a nightdress appearing to be fresh.

PARSONS. You know about her mother?


**WILLIAM** (*eleven*) *and* **CONSTANCE** (*twelve*) *by the side of the road to Bath.*

**WILLIAM. Are you sure this is the right way?**

**CONSTANCE. Can't you smell the salt in the air?**

   **WILLIAM** *breathes in.*

**WILLIAM** (*smiling*). **Not salt.**

**CONSTANCE. Not my fault if you never bathe.**

**WILLIAM. I wouldn't care if we got lost anyway.**

**CONSTANCE. Sooner we get to Bristol sooner we can be cabin boys and escape this place.**

**WILLIAM. Mother liked to get lost.**

**CONSTANCE. She couldn't help it.**

**WILLIAM. She liked it. She told me once.**

**CONSTANCE. She was mentally disturbed, William.**

**WILLIAM. That's what Pa said. He said she gets lost while walking with her children near our home, she must be mad, but she told me that was when she was most happy. She told me she loved having my hand in hers, walking in the sunshine, on familiar paths, for as long as she could. And when she was gone too long she told them she'd got lost, but she did it on purpose.**

**CONSTANCE. I never walked with her.**

**WILLIAM. She wanted you to.**

*Pause.*

**I wouldn't mind if we got lost.**

*He holds his hand out to* **CONSTANCE.** *After a moment she takes it.*


PARSONS. There is a theory that simply brooding on one's hereditary taint of madness can bring it on. Wilkie Collins uses it in one of his stories, I happened to know him as well while I was in London, but perhaps the imaginings of this country's greatest writers are of no interest to a man of your profession. Do you call it a profession?

WHICHER. Let us stick to what you found in the post-mortem, doctor. Had the boy been drugged?

PARSONS. We opened his stomach, but didn't detect anything.

Mrs Kent asked me to certify the girl as a lunatic, did you know that?

WHICHER. The post-mortem

PARSONS. Very well, the stab to his chest was a bit more than an inch wide, it'd pushed the heart out of place, / punctured the diaphragm and grazed the outer edge of // the stomach. Yes, it would have required very great force to inflict such a blow, but I have no doubt Miss Constance is strong enough to have inflicted it.


CONSTANCE. / We don't need to

// We don't need to

WHICHER. Did you really do this, all this, alone?

CONSTANCE. The corridors at Millbank lead to more corridors, you can't tell what time of day it is, you could walk those corridors for years and never get anywhere.

What I did to Saville, an innocent boy, what was done to my mother, what has been done to the women in this prison and all the prisons I've been in, at Millbank I worked in the infirmary and the scars I saw, the things that had been done to them, the things we do to one another, Mr Whicher, are unfathomable.

WHICHER. I am charging you with the murder of your brother, Francis Saville Kent, on the early morning of Saturday the thirtieth of June this year.

CONSTANCE. I am innocent.

MR KENT. I would have appreciated some warning, detective.

CONSTANCE. Pa, I am innocent.

WHICHER. We shall go to the Temperance Hall in Road where I will request that you be remanded while I continue my investigation.

MR KENT. Where will she be remanded?

WHICHER. The gaol at Devizes.

MR KENT. Will she be looked after?

WHICHER. It is a gaol, Mr Kent.

MR KENT. You think she is guilty?

WHICHER. It's what you yourself believe.

MR KENT. But you're a professional, you've encountered more criminals than I ever will, and you believe she is capable?

WHICHER. I need more than belief, without evidence my suspicions mean nothing.

MR KENT. Remanding my sixteen-year-old daughter isn't nothing, detective. Guilty or not, that isn't nothing. What if I'm wrong, what if we're wrong, what future will she have?

WHICHER. Saville was denied a future, it helps me to remember that.

CONSTANCE *feels something in her pocket. She takes out a small child's sock. She looks at* WHICHER, *confused.*

CONSTANCE. I've been given needlework shifts, I must've

*She examines the sock.*

WHICHER. What did you feel when I arrested you? When I addressed the magistrates and asked for you to be remanded, you didn't say anything, you didn't express any emotion whatsoever, a girl of sixteen.

CONSTANCE. What did you want me to say?

*She continues to be preoccupied by the sock.*

WHICHER. I admit, the arrest was something of a ruse, I thought it would shock you into a confession. I'd done it before and it had worked on grown men, but you held your nerve.


*April 1856.* **MRS KENT** (*thirty-six*) *holds a baby.* **CONSTANCE** (*twelve*) *stands in the corner, crying.*

**MRS KENT. If it weren't for me you would've remained at school for the holidays, no one else is interested in you, Constance, no one else wanted to see you.**

**CONSTANCE. I want to be good, I do, I do.**

**MRS KENT. I see no evidence of that. Now get out, I'm sick of the sight of you already.**


WHICHER. That week I carried out a thorough investigation but I knew the chances of finding your nightdress were long gone, and that was the only sure evidence. I was left with the tenuous recollections of schoolgirls like Louisa Hatherill.


HATHERILL. Is it true she's in gaol?

WHICHER. She's on remand.

HATHERILL. Which means in gaol, doesn't it?

WHICHER. For a week, yes.

HATHERILL. I don't know what I'd do in gaol, probably cry all the time, but she'll fight her corner, Constance, I wouldn't worry about her. She loves to wrestle, she likes playing Heenan and Sayers.

WHICHER. The boxers?

HATHERILL. None of us want to fight her but she loves showing off how strong she is. We'd all be happy to take her word for it and she's proved it enough times.

WHICHER. You said she's spoken to you about the younger children at home.

HATHERILL. She said her parents favoured them, and how her brother had to wheel the perambulator for the young ones and he didn't like doing it.

WHICHER. Did she say anything else?

HATHERILL. How she heard her father comparing William and Saville, saying what a much finer man Saville would be.


WHICHER. William's doing very well for himself.

CONSTANCE. I knew he would.

WHICHER. I read he's curator at the Royal Aquarium, which sounds impressive.

CONSTANCE. He's a passionate scientist.

WHICHER. Do you think he's grateful?

CONSTANCE. Why should he be grateful, he earned it, do you think it came easily?

WHICHER. Grateful to you.

CONSTANCE. He has no reason to be.

*Pause.*

WHICHER. Why didn't you kill Eveline? She was only one, she was sleeping in the same room, wouldn't it have been easier to carry her all the way to the privy? Why Saville?

CONSTANCE. He was their favourite.

WHICHER. They doted on all the children. Killing any of them would've had the desired effect.

Was it because he was the only boy, other than William?

CONSTANCE. He was their favourite.

WHICHER. William became the only surviving son. No one to be compared to.


**WILLIAM. I wouldn't mind if we got lost.**

**WILLIAM (*eleven*) *holds his hand out to* CONSTANCE (*twelve*). *After a moment she takes it.***


CONSTANCE. When we were walking to Bristol, William and I, the time we ran away to be cabin boys, I pretended to get us lost. I knew the way, it wasn't a difficult route, but I took us down a wrong path deliberately and pretended we were lost.

WHICHER. Why?

CONSTANCE. We had to climb through hawthorn. He didn't complain. We both loved adventure, we were still children.

WHICHER. You were exceptionally composed for a child.

CONSTANCE. But I was a child, Mr Whicher.

Even when I killed Saville, I was still only sixteen.

WHICHER. You conducted yourself very maturely.

The way you concealed the bloodstained nightdress took the upmost composure.

CONSTANCE. The hardest part was over by then.

WHICHER. Miss Cox, does anyone else help with the laundry, other than Mary Ann and Elizabeth?

COX. No, it's my job.

WHICHER. Miss Constance doesn't help?

COX. No.

She came to the lumber room that day, but it wasn't to help, she'd lost her purse and wanted me to check if it was in her slip pocket.

WHICHER. So you checked the slip pocket for her?

COX. Of course. I took her slip out of the basket to check the pocket, but her purse wasn't there.

WHICHER. So you returned the slip to the basket and she went in search of her purse elsewhere?

COX. She asked me to get her a glass of water.

WHICHER. So you left her in the lumber room alone?

COX. She stood at the top of the stairs and waited for me.

WHICHER. How long were you gone?

COX. A minute? It's only down the stairs.


**WILLIAM** (*eleven*) *and* **CONSTANCE** (*twelve*) *walk to Bath.*

**WILLIAM. What would you do if you saw a pirate?**

**CONSTANCE. First of all I'd hide.**

**WILLIAM. Where?**

**CONSTANCE. Below deck.**

**WILLIAM. Then what?**

**CONSTANCE. I'd let them think everyone on board the ship was dead. And then just as they were relaxing**

**WILLIAM. We'd burst out from our hiding place and**

**CONSTANCE. We'd sneak up on them**

**WILLIAM. And, and we'd stab them**

**CONSTANCE. And pour hot tar over them**

**WILLIAM. And, and, and throw them in the sea**

**CONSTANCE. And watch them drown.**

**They'd do the same to you.**

WHICHER. You asked Miss Cox to look for your purse so she'd unpack the laundry and you could see where your nightdress was. Then, when she went downstairs to get you a glass of water, you stole it back from the basket. This isn't the bloodstained nightdress, no, you destroyed that one. This was a clean nightdress you'd only worn for one night, but you needed it to seem like one of your nightdresses had been lost by the washerwoman. Then no one would miss the bloodied one you'd already destroyed.

You weren't panicking. This is a clever plan. You divert attention outside the house, away from yourself.

CONSTANCE. Why is it a surprise that I should come up with a clever plan?

People underestimated me.

Did they underestimate you?

Is that why this case haunts you?

It's not about justice, or the Truth, or anything as noble as that, it's that you failed and they lost faith in you after everything you'd had to do to make a name for yourself.

WHICHER. I deserve the truth.

CONSTANCE. Deserve it?

WHICHER. I was denounced in parliament.

I was held up as everything that was wrong with the Metropolitan police. I was reviled for arresting you, a young lady.

Newspapers across the country said my witchery had jeopardised your future, yours? They said I was motivated by greed, I wanted the reward.

CONSTANCE. What was written or said about you had nothing to do with me.

WHICHER. They rallied in your defence.

CONSTANCE. I never courted the public's attention.

WHICHER. But you had it.

Spectators were spilling out of Temperance Hall, they were selling stereoscopic cards of your home, books were written.

CONSTANCE. You can accuse me of many things, but you can't say I courted the public's attention. It's the last thing I wanted. I wore a veil over my face that day at Temperance Hall.

WHICHER. Maybe you wanted to be an enigma.

CONSTANCE. You ask anyone in this prison, any prison I've been in, I don't speak about my crime, I have no interest in entertaining people or satisfying their curiosity or any of the other things they might want from me.

Mr Edlin might've been looking to entertain the masses, but his approach was nothing to do with me.


EDLIN. Let me begin, sirs, by asking that you instantly liberate Miss Constance Kent, for there is not one tittle of evidence against this young lady.

An atrocious murder has been committed, but I am afraid that it has been followed by a judicial murder of a scarcely less atrocious character.

It will never, never be forgotten that this young lady has

been dragged from her home and sent like a common felon, a common vagrant, to Devizes Gaol. This step ought to have been taken only after the most mature consideration and after something like tangible evidence, and not upon the fact that a paltry bedgown was missing. Its loss is careless, / but nothing more sinister. // No doubt can remain that this little peg, upon which this fearful charge has been hung, has well and truly fallen to the ground.

WHICHER. / It wasn't lost.

// You tricked them.

EDLIN. The steps you have taken will be such as to ruin her for life, every hope is gone with regard to this young girl. And where is the evidence?

The one fact is the suspicion of Mr Whicher, a man eager in the pursuit of the murderer and anxious for the reward that has been offered.

He was baffled and annoyed by not finding a clue and has caught at that which was no clue at all.

WHICHER. What am I but a working-class man meddling in a respectable family's affairs? How on earth could I possibly understand the motivations and passions of beings so far above my station?

And so they release you, and you return to Road Hill House.

CONSTANCE. That wasn't easy.

WHICHER. Surely it was preferable to proceeding to a murder trial?

**MR KENT** (*fifty-nine*) *and* **MRS KENT** (*forty*), *who is very heavily pregnant, are in the library.* **CONSTANCE** (*sixteen*) *enters.*

**MRS KENT. I never want to see her again.**

**MR KENT. I asked her to come in, Mary. We will have to find a way to exist alongside one another for now.**

**MRS KENT.** Why are you looking at me? Don't look at me.

She belongs in a cage, Samuel.

**CONSTANCE.** Like my mother?

**MRS KENT.** Don't speak to me.

I don't know what you are but it's unnatural whatever it is, you're a monster.

I don't care what they found, I know, I've always known.

**MR KENT.** We will stay in separate quarters, you won't have to see her.

**MRS KENT.** She could do it again, Samuel, are you so weak-minded?

My dearest boy, my innocent, my Saville, my

*She looks directly at* **CONSTANCE** *and screams.*


CONSTANCE *is shaken.*

WHICHER. How did William respond to your return?

CONSTANCE. William?

WHICHER. Constance, are you well?


*The family group pray together on the evening of 29th June 1860.*

**MR KENT.** Father, whose nature and property is ever to have mercy and to forgive, receive our humble petitions; and though we be tied and bound with the chain of our sins, yet let the pitifulness of thy great mercy loose us

*As* **MR KENT** *speaks every member of the household present turns to stare at* **CONSTANCE**. *They each put on a mask of Saville's face.*

CONSTANCE. This is about your pride, not Truth. You're a proud man who feels hard done by, that's the truth. You force me to go through / it yet again

WHICHER. I never forced / you to

CONSTANCE. as if it hasn't plagued me every day since it happened. On the promise of a letter, when the truth is your word, your recommendation isn't worth the paper it's written on, and the fact you think it would still mean something only shows the extent of your delusion. You have no influence, Mr Whicher, you have no standing, no sway, no clout, and you've come to the wrong person if you're looking for consolation.

WHICHER. William has influence. William has standing and sway and everything he wanted.

CONSTANCE. Why don't you visit him, then?

WHICHER. Why do you protect him?

CONSTANCE. Please

**MISS PRATT. She belongs in an asylum.**

**MR KENT (*laughing*). Shhh.**

**MISS PRATT. A cage.**

CONSTANCE. I'm where I should be.

I always thought I could be good

but I'm as deluded as you are, Mr Whicher.

(*Calls out.*) Guard.

WHICHER. Wait, Constance. I know it's difficult, what I'm asking, but we are getting somewhere.

CONSTANCE. Getting where?

GUARD *appears.*

**WILLIAM** (*eleven*) *and* **CONSTANCE** (*twelve*).

**WILLIAM. my hand in hers, walking in the sunshine, on familiar paths, for as long as she could. And when she was gone too long she told them she'd got lost, but she did it on purpose.**

CONSTANCE. This is where I belong, that's the Truth. Take it.

WHICHER. Constance, please, I'm not deluded, I know there's more to this story.

CONSTANCE. It's not a story, you're right. I murdered Saville. That's not a story.

WHICHER. There's more to it though, I know it.

This isn't about my pride, about restoring other people's faith in me, none of that matters now, I need

*Pause.*

Have I wasted my time?

CONSTANCE. I can't help you with that.

*Pause.*

GUARD. Sir?

WHICHER *exits with* GUARD, *leaving* CONSTANCE *on stage alone.*

BOY *walks into the space. They watch each other.*

## ACT TWO

*Fulham Prison, a few weeks later.*

CONSTANCE. I'd found a way to exist. I never speak about my crime. I don't seek out company. But these past few weeks, I can't get back to, since speaking to you, I can't

BOY *enters and distracts* CONSTANCE *by offering her a bead ring he has made. She rejects it.*

I will never forgive myself for what I did to him.

*Pause.*

Aren't you going to launch into more questions?

WHICHER *shakes his head.*

But you came back.

WHICHER *nods.*

WHICHER *takes out a piece of paper and offers it to her.*

*She takes it and reads.*

The list of my linen, when I came back from school that June. You still have this?

It didn't prove anything.

WHICHER. No.

CONSTANCE. But you held onto it?

WHICHER. I don't want to disturb what equilibrium you've managed to find, Constance. Going over the events again doesn't change them.

CONSTANCE. What happened to treading carefully and paying attention to the details?

WHICHER. It didn't work. My methods haven't worked. A list of linen won't provide any answers. Keep it.

CONSTANCE. Why would I want it?

WHICHER. Throw it away then.

CONSTANCE. You're giving up?

WHICHER. If you want to put it like that.

CONSTANCE. How would you put it?

WHICHER. I would say there are secrets you have no intention of ever sharing with anyone, and there probably isn't anything I can do to change that.

CONSTANCE. Probably?

WHICHER. The approaches I have taken in the past have failed.

CONSTANCE. Why are you so certain there's anything more to know?

WHICHER. I'm not certain.

CONSTANCE. Then why did you come back?

WHICHER. Why did you ask me back?

*Pause.*

CONSTANCE. You said I wanted to be an enigma. I've never wanted that.

WHICHER. My mistake.

CONSTANCE. You said you were denounced in parliament. I'm sorry for that. When I think about all the damage I've done, it's overwhelming but I know I have done good

WHICHER. For William?

CONSTANCE. And I try to focus on the good I could do. If I can help you understand, Mr Whicher, then I'll try.

*Pause.*

You asked what it was like when I came back home.

That's when I realised how much had changed. Not just within our family, but there were endless articles about the case, the public couldn't get enough of the tragedy, I started to see that it was beyond control.

*October, 1860.*

CONSTANCE. Haven't they got anything else to write about?

WILLIAM. They'll lose interest.

CONSTANCE. What does your appearance have to do with anything? Why should you be 'strong looking'?

WILLIAM. At least it means I'm not a suspect.

CONSTANCE. Not a suspect maybe, but only because they say you're weak and effeminate. They want to make sure not a single one of us comes out of this with any prospects.

WILLIAM. It's not the worst thing to be written.

CONSTANCE. And why are they dragging Miss Gough through the mud?

WILLIAM. The magistrates released her.

CONSTANCE. But how will she find work now? Who'll employ her?

WILLIAM. She can live with her family.

CONSTANCE. What would've happened if they'd found her guilty?

WILLIAM. They won't.

CONSTANCE. Don't you care?

WILLIAM. There's no evidence against her.

CONSTANCE. They still arrested her. Apparently they don't need evidence to completely destroy someone's life.

WILLIAM. She won't starve.

CONSTANCE. She was always kind to Saville, she doesn't deserve to be caught up in this. What would've happened if they'd

WILLIAM. Stop, Connie.

CONSTANCE. If Miss Gough ended up in gaol, or worse, because she happened to work for / our family.

WILLIAM. She won't.


WHICHER. Did William know of your guilt?

CONSTANCE *shakes her head*.

So what did he think had happened?

CONSTANCE. I can't speak for him.

WHICHER. He was confident Miss Gough wasn't responsible.

CONSTANCE. I really don't know what he thought.

WHICHER. You said you'd try to help me understand. I find it difficult to believe you never discussed between you what happened.


*A* CROWD *of people gather at the gate, shouting. The lines are shouted by different members of the crowd, over the top of each other.*

CROWD. Who murdered the boy?

CONSTANCE. Why can't they leave us alone?

CROWD. That's her, Constance Kent!

CONSTANCE (*shouts*). Leave us alone.

CROWD. Who killed Saville?

WILLIAM. Let's go inside.

CONSTANCE. This is our garden, why should we hide?

CROWD. Child murderers!

CONSTANCE (*shouts*). Haven't we suffered enough?

WILLIAM. It won't make any difference, Connie.

CROWD. Fratricide!

WILLIAM. They know nothing.

CONSTANCE. We'll never be free of this, we'll never be free until someone pays.

CROWD. Did you kill your brother, Constance?

CONSTANCE. Already at school you say the masters don't trust you. There's not a man, woman or child in England who doesn't know who we are.

CROWD. Are you protecting your father, William?

CONSTANCE. They might not all stand at our gates shouting, but they think it and they'll never stop thinking it until someone pays.

CROWD. He was an angel!

WILLIAM. I'm not listening to this.

CROWD. Shame on you!

WILLIAM *tries to go inside.*

CONSTANCE. Don't run away, William, it looks weak!

CROWD. Who killed the child?

WILLIAM. Why should I stand here and listen to them?

*As he walks away* CONSTANCE *grabs him and pulls him back forcefully.*

CONSTANCE. Stay!

WILLIAM. That hurt.

CONSTANCE. Don't run away.

WILLIAM. Don't do that again.

CONSTANCE. Do you want to look weak?

CROWD. We're watching you!

CONSTANCE. Don't let it affect you.

WILLIAM. They can say what they like, I don't have to listen to it.

*He walks away again and she pulls him back, except this time he resists, pushing her away so she falls.*

CROWD. Murderers!

CONSTANCE. You're not weak, William.

*He's standing over her, but doesn't offer to help her up.*

WILLIAM. I know I'm not.

CROWD. Why did you do it?

WILLIAM. Imagine having nothing better to do with your day than shouting at strangers.

CONSTANCE. Show them we're not afraid, William, stay.

WILLIAM *walks back to the house.*

CROWD. What happened to the nightdress?

CONSTANCE *stays sitting on the grass, absorbing the crowd's abuse.*

Was he awake when you did it?

Shame!

The Lord will punish you.

What did you do with the dagger?

Cowards!


CONSTANCE. My mother wasn't weak, William's never been weak and neither have I.

Eventually my father sent me to Dinan in France. I suppose he didn't know what else to do with me.

*Dinan, France*. DENIS *(four) appears. He is making a nest out of twigs and leaves*. CONSTANCE *(seventeen) watches him*.

CONSTANCE. You're very good at building nests.

DENIS *looks at her, he doesn't understand, he only speaks French*.

*(Indicates the nest.)* Nest.

DENIS. Nid.

CONSTANCE. Nid. C'est bon.

Are you a bird?

*He doesn't understand*.

*(Flaps her arms.)* Oiseau.

DENIS *(points at the nest)*. Nid.

*He continues to gather materials*.

*She picks up a twig and offers it to him. He examines it*.

C'est trop grand.

*He drops the twig*.

CONSTANCE. You're busy. Saville was always busy. Always had something to show me. A bead ring he'd made. A stick he'd found. A song he'd learned. It was easy to like him.

I'm not easy to like.

No one here likes me.

Apart from you, Denis, and even our friendship is probably one-sided.

But I don't mind honesty. They don't like me and they make it clear, I can accept that. What I can't accept, what I can't allow is pretence. Is being made to feel you are loved only to learn you were a substitute. Until the real thing arrived. That the love you felt was real, was not.

They sent me here to be finished.

I'm already finished.

Not in the way they would like.

It's difficult to see how my life continues from here.

Maybe that's as it should be.

Saville's life doesn't continue.

Who will you be, Denis?

A great engineer perhaps.

DENIS *has finished the nest. He picks it up and offers it to* CONSTANCE.

DENIS. Pour vous.

*She takes it and is overcome.*

CONSTANCE. Merci.

DENIS. Un nid, pour vous.

CONSTANCE. Une maison.

DENIS. Non, un nid.

CONSTANCE. Oui. Un nid.


WHICHER. I was sent to Poland. Not the same as France, but

CONSTANCE. Were they trying to get rid of you?

WHICHER. The Russians wanted advice on how to set up a detective service. They were worried about Polish nationalists. There'd been assassination attempts on the Tsar's family.

CONSTANCE. And the Metropolitan Police sent you? They must've still had faith in you.

WHICHER. Six months or so after our visit the Russians were shooting insurgents. Questions were asked in the House of Commons about the ethics of our mission.

I left the police a year after that.

CONSTANCE. Why?

WHICHER. Too many doubts. My mind was

The truth had become something that was

unstable, uncertain, un

CONSTANCE. Perhaps you went mad.

WHICHER. Perhaps.

CONSTANCE. But no one used that word to describe you, did they?

You retired, got your pension.

WHICHER *nods*.

*Pause*.

They left me in France for two years. Then my father and William came to see me.

*1863*. MR KENT (*sixty-two*) *and* WILLIAM (*eighteen*) *enter*.

CONSTANCE. Is it as you imagined?

WILLIAM. Everything's as you said in your letters. The port, the streets, it's medieval, like the town time forgot.

CONSTANCE. Feels like I've been banished to another world.

MR KENT. No one banished you.

CONSTANCE. You didn't want me near.

MR KENT. It's a beautiful town. The convent has been an edifying place to be. This wasn't punishment. You were better off here.

CONSTANCE. Away from my family.

MR KENT. I can tell you about punishment, Constance, I can tell you about pain that never ends, guilt that will never end.

CONSTANCE. Guilt?

MR KENT. This, Constance, this peaceful life you've been leading is not punishment.

*Pause.*

CONSTANCE. How's life in Llangollen?

MR KENT. It goes on. We're generally left alone, I can carry out my duties there, it became impossible in England.

CONSTANCE. How is Mamma?

MR KENT. Do you really want to know?

CONSTANCE. And my new sister, Florence?

MR KENT. She's growing strong.

CONSTANCE. It's hard to believe I've never met her.

MR KENT. It may well be some years until you do.

CONSTANCE. Am I not welcome in Llangollen?

*Pause.*

WILLIAM. Do you have access to the new thinking here?

CONSTANCE. Pa?

WILLIAM. Have you had the opportunity to read Mr Darwin's work?

CONSTANCE. I'm not sure the nuns of Dinan are ready for that.

WILLIAM. As soon as I read it, Connie, I knew what I wanted to do with my life. Mr Darwin's new science is the most exciting, mind-expanding field you could hope to work in, uncovering the very origins and nature of life on this planet.

CONSTANCE. You'll do great things, William.

WILLIAM. Will I have the opportunity, that's the question. William Kent of the infamous Road Hill House.

MR KENT. You'll be moving back to England.

CONSTANCE. When?

MR KENT. In a few days. You'll journey back with us.

CONSTANCE. So I will meet Florence?

MR KENT. You'll be going to St Mary's in Brighton. I want you to think of it as a new life.

CONSTANCE. Brighton? That's nowhere near Llangollen.

MR KENT. No.

CONSTANCE. So then I may as well be in France.

MR KENT. I can't continue to pay for your upkeep here.

CONSTANCE. So it's a financial decision.

MR KENT. It's a financial necessity, Constance. There isn't a single element of life that has been unaffected, we must live more frugally.

CONSTANCE. Will you visit?

MR KENT. I want you to think of St Mary's as your new family.

CONSTANCE. My new family?

MR KENT. A religious order is a kind of family.

It's the natural way of things, Constance, as children grow they establish families of their own.

CONSTANCE. Mary Ann and Elizabeth haven't. William hasn't.

MR KENT. I could've written but I wanted to see you.

CONSTANCE. One last time.

MR KENT. We must each adapt to our circumstances. Unless we adapt, we will not survive. That's one of Mr Darwin's theories, is it not?

WILLIAM. He talks about change over millions of years.

MR KENT. Well, sometimes it must be done much quicker. We leave for Brighton the day after tomorrow. You'll settle into your new home, Constance. We all have to adapt.

WHICHER. You were treated differently to William. To the rest of the family.

CONSTANCE. My father believed I was guilty. He did his best to see as little of me as possible, but he couldn't quite forsake me. Maybe even he saw some good in me.

**EDWARD** (*eighteen*) *and* **MR KENT** (*fifty-two*).

**EDWARD. And what do you think killed her?**

**MR KENT. An obstruction of the bowel.**

**EDWARD. You don't think it killed her to have to live in this house with you and her carrying on so brazenly? The servants knew it, everyone did, that's why we've had to move so often.**

WHICHER. And what of your new family at St Mary's?

CONSTANCE. Reverend Wagner has been a constant in my life since then.

WAGNER. A warm welcome to you, Constance.

CONSTANCE. I go by Emilie now.

WAGNER. A change in name can be a helpful way to express a greater change within ourselves.

CONSTANCE. It was my middle name.

WAGNER. Ties to the past are important too.

How are you finding life in our community?

CONSTANCE. Like family.

WAGNER. Family is not simple.

The Lord said unto Cain, where is Abel, thy brother? And he said, I know not, am I my brother's keeper? And He said, what hast thou done? The voice of thy brother's blood crieth unto me from the ground.

Family is not simple.

The children born here at our hospital for unmarried mothers will know that from the moment they know anything at all, others learn it later, but we all learn it at some point.

When did you learn it, Emilie?

*Pause.*

CONSTANCE. Perhaps it was when my mother died.

My father wronged her. But I only came to see that when it was too late.


**CONSTANCE** (*five*).

**CONSTANCE. and she went quiet, and so I said, have you got a problem with your ears, too, and she didn't say anything, so I said, have you got a problem with your tongue as well and she stayed quiet, so I said, and you wonder why I prefer my other Mamma?**


CONSTANCE. I wronged her, too.

WAGNER. Blood ties are as fluid and unstable as the stuff they're made of. Our religious family offers something far more solid and lasting. A place where the truth is known and should never be feared because forgiveness is given. Confess and forgiveness is given.

You're part of our family now, Emilie.


WHICHER. Do you think your father chose St Mary's deliberately?

CONSTANCE. What, because I've always liked the sea?

WHICHER. Reverend Wagner is a well-known member of the Anglo-Catholic movement. He supports the revival of sacramental confession in the Anglican Church, doesn't he?

CONSTANCE. It was a safe place for me to be. What were my options? Not marriage. Not an education or a career of my own. Where would you put me?

*Brighton beach, March 1865.* WILLIAM (*nineteen*) *and* CONSTANCE (*twenty-one*).

WILLIAM. I wonder if pirates ever came ashore here.

CONSTANCE. What made you think of that?

WILLIAM. Don't you remember our obsession with pirates?

CONSTANCE. I wouldn't call it an obsession.

WILLIAM. We ran away to sea together.

CONSTANCE. To be cabin boys, not pirates.

WILLIAM. True.

CONSTANCE. Far more law-abiding.

WILLIAM. Not that we made it. But that didn't matter. I've had some of the happiest days of my life with you, Connie.

Now I look at this beach and I wonder what natural treasures are buried here, yet to be discovered. What geological wonders, what clues about the progression of our species and this earth.

CONSTANCE. I see a lot of pebbles.

WILLIAM. You must see more than that.

CONSTANCE *looks at him.*

CONSTANCE. You at my side.

WILLIAM. Always.

*Pause.*

This stretch of coast probably isn't as interesting as the cliffs of Hampshire, they're packed with fossils.

It's my life's calling, Connie. To discover things. To make our family name synonymous with scientific learning, not the death of a boy.

CONSTANCE. Murder.

WILLIAM. The murder of a boy.

But you were right, you always are. There will for ever be a cloud over me and I won't be permitted to progress in the career I was meant to have. It's just as you said. Until someone admits guilt, I have no future.

*The sound of the sea on the pebbles.*

*A train from Brighton to Victoria Station, London.*

CONSTANCE, REVEREND WAGNER *and* KATHARINE GREAM *sit in a carriage.* GREAM, *Lady Superior of St Mary's, wears a long black cloak with a high white frill,* WAGNER *is in his vicar's garb.* CONSTANCE *wears a loose veil. They make an austere trio.*

CONSTANCE *picks at the armrest intermittently, which starts to irritate* GREAM.

*A* PASSENGER *enters and sits in an empty seat, but after a short time, senses something strange in the air and moves seats.*

*Other passengers walk past, clock the party, or don't notice them at all.*

*Bow Street Magistrates' court.* THOMAS HENRY *reads her letter.* CONSTANCE *is next to* WAGNER *and* GREAM.

HENRY. It is my duty to ask if any inducement has been made to the prisoner in any way to make this confession.

WAGNER. None whatever has been made by me. It was entirely her own proposition that she should be taken before a London magistrate.

HENRY. Whatever you say must be entirely your own free and voluntary statement. No inducement that may have been held out to you is to have any effect upon your mind.

CONSTANCE. No inducement ever has, sir.

HENRY. I must remind you that it is the most serious crime that can be committed and that your statement will be used against you at your trial. (*Lifts up the letter*.) This is the paper you wish to hand in as your statement.

HENRY *hands the letter to* CONSTANCE.

Please read it.

CONSTANCE (*reads the statement*). I, Constance Emilie Kent, alone and unaided on the night of the twenty-ninth of June eighteen sixty, murdered at Road Hill House, Wiltshire, Francis Saville Kent. Before the deed none knew of my intention, nor after of my guilt. No one assisted me in the crime, nor in my evasion of discovery.

HENRY. Do you wish to sign it?

CONSTANCE. Yes.

HENRY *hands her a pen and she signs it*.

HENRY. I shall be committing you for trial.


WHICHER. Did you tell William you planned to confess?

CONSTANCE *shakes her head*.

But you did it for him?

CONSTANCE. I did it for myself, my own conscience.

WHICHER. You knew it was a capital case.

CONSTANCE *nods*.

You were willing to die, so that he might pursue a fulfilling career?

It's courageous.

MR KENT (*sixty-four*) *and* CONSTANCE (*twenty-one*) *in Devizes Gaol. He holds her. It is a complete embrace, neither wants it to end.*

CONSTANCE. I'd learned to pray by then, God told me this was the right thing to do.

WHICHER. Some people thought there were papist forces at work in your confession.

CONSTANCE. If some people find prayer sinister I can't help that.

Did you feel vindicated by my confession?

WHICHER. I knew you were guilty. But you'd got away with it, so I was surprised. I thought it'd be a deathbed job.

MR KENT *and* CONSTANCE *in Devizes Gaol.*

CONSTANCE. I'm not mad.

MR KENT. I know you're not.

CONSTANCE. Nor was my mother.

MR KENT. You didn't see her at her worst, we protected you from it.

CONSTANCE. You didn't protect me, Pa.

*Silence.*

MR KENT. I can't protect you from this.

CONSTANCE. I don't expect you to.

MR KENT. I've arranged for meals to be provided, and I'll visit as often as they allow, but I can't protect you from

WHICHER. You spoke with Doctor Bucknill while you were at Devizes Gaol. What did he ask you?

CONSTANCE. He wanted an account of how I killed Saville.

CONSTANCE. A few days before the murder, I took a razor from my father's case and hid it. This is the only weapon I used.

I hid a candle and matches in the corner of the privy.

On the night of the murder I undressed and went to bed, in case my sisters visited my room.

When I thought everyone was asleep, I went downstairs and opened the drawing-room door and shutters.

I went to the nursery, took Saville out of his cot.

WHICHER. And managed to fold back the bedclothes neatly?

CONSTANCE. I carried him downstairs to the drawing room and opened the window.

WHICHER. While holding Saville, a child of nearly four?

CONSTANCE. I climbed out, went round the house and into the closet. I lit the candle and put it on the seat of the closet. Then I cut his throat. The blood didn't come, and I didn't think he was dead, so I stuck the razor in his side and put the body in the vault.

I went back to my bedroom and there were two spots of blood on my nightdress.

WHICHER. How was it only two spots of blood when you'd stabbed the boy?

CONSTANCE. I washed them out in the basin and threw the water into the footpan. I took another nightdress and got into bed.

WHICHER. Did you sleep?

CONSTANCE. The constables examined my nightdresses the next day but they didn't see any stains, even though I could see them when I looked later. So I hid it, in case they were more thorough next time, and I burnt it in my bedroom fireplace five or six days later.

WHICHER. Doctor Bucknill thought you had inherited a strong tendency to insanity.

CONSTANCE. I wouldn't let him state his belief in public. And in any case, I wasn't mad. Did you think I was?

WHICHER. I'm not the eminent alienist.

CONSTANCE. But you have an opinion.

*Pause.*

I've never hidden behind an insanity plea, even though others advised me to.

WHICHER. At the trial the judge asked how do you plead and you said Guilty. When he asked you again there was a long pause.

CONSTANCE. I knew what it meant.

WHICHER. The judge put on his black cap and said you appear to have allowed feelings of jealousy and / anger to have

CONSTANCE. Not jealousy.

I wasn't jealous of Saville. I was angry, yes, I was furious,
I was full of hate towards a woman who'd pretended to love
me, who'd used me, who had denied me the chance to know
my real mother, the one who did love me.

WHICHER. He told you you were to be hanged.

But the public turned. There was a swell of sympathy for
you, calls for you to be spared. Eminent men of science and
the law, even the judge himself, all rallied in support for you,
petitioning the Home Secretary to commute your sentence to
penal servitude for life.

CONSTANCE. They were squeamish about my youth. My
confession probably counted for something. And I wasn't
a threat to the public. I'm not, a threat.

WHICHER. But you deserved to be punished.

CONSTANCE. No question.

WHICHER. Doesn't William, too?

*Pause.*

CONSTANCE. I've told you things I haven't told anyone else,
but that's all there is.

WHICHER. I believe both you and William murdered Saville.

I believe you sacrificed yourself for William.

That's the Truth, isn't it?

*Pause.*

I have no interest in pursuing William, that's in the hands of
a higher power than me, I just want to know

CONSTANCE. You said you wanted to understand, well I can
only tell you about myself. What I have done.

WHICHER. But if you did it together, Constance, then you
know what he's done, too.

CONSTANCE. Don't ask me about William, Mr Whicher, and I won't ask you about the child you lost.

*Silence.*

*He nods.*

WHICHER. I can write you the letter if you want.

I can't promise it'll help.

CONSTANCE. Thank you.

*He exits.*

## EPILOGUE

*1895. An Institute for Young Offenders in Parramatta, on the outskirts of Sydney, Australia. The reception room. There are windows, looking out over a garden.*

EMILIE (*fifty-one*) *opens the door.*

EMILIE. I don't think there's anyone in here.

No, come in.

OLDER WILLIAM (*fifty*) *enters.*

OLDER WILLIAM. I would've gone to your home, but you're never there.

EMILIE. I'm usually here.

OLDER WILLIAM. Exactly, I thought it my best bet.

EMILIE. Can I get you something to drink?

OLDER WILLIAM. No, you're working, I won't stay long.

(*Looks around.*) I'm glad to see it, I can picture you here when I'm back in England. I'm pleased you're not at the lepers' colony any more, that wasn't a pretty picture.

EMILIE. It's a good change.

OLDER WILLIAM. I was surprised though.

EMILIE. Why?

OLDER WILLIAM. They aren't sick, in the traditional sense.

EMILIE. They don't have typhoid or leprosy, no, but I think I can help.

OLDER WILLIAM. I have no doubt of that, but it is a change.

EMILIE. You've moved jobs more than anyone I know.
Tasmania, Melbourne, Brisbane, London, / Perth

OLDER WILLIAM. Yes, but always within the same field, / always

EMILIE. I consider this a related field.

OLDER WILLIAM. Young offenders? They don't need a nurse, a gaoler, maybe.

EMILIE. Have you come here to lecture me, William?

OLDER WILLIAM. I know better than to do that.

I don't like to think of you anywhere near a gaol, you served your time.

EMILIE. This isn't a gaol.

When do you leave for England?

OLDER WILLIAM. Next week.

We plan to settle in Hampshire. The cliffs there are packed with fossils.

EMILIE. I remember you saying.

OLDER WILLIAM. I do go on, sorry. Plenty for me to do. And there's the new book to write.

EMILIE. Will you be back?

OLDER WILLIAM. I hope so.

I was packing up yesterday, making difficult decisions about which animals I can take with me, and I remembered those two tropical birds Edward sent us, we were probably nine and ten, do you remember those?

EMILIE. The brightest coloured feathers I'd ever seen.

OLDER WILLIAM. I forget where they were from, somewhere in the Caribbean perhaps.

EMILIE. She made us keep them in a cold back room and they died.

OLDER WILLIAM. I thought that was what happened.

*Pause.*

I thank God every day I had you.

EMILIE. Do you pray, William?

OLDER WILLIAM. What kind of question's that?

EMILIE. I hope you do.

*Pause.*

Your success brings me more happiness than anything else.

OLDER WILLIAM. Any success I've had is down to you.

NURSE *enters.*

NURSE. Excuse me, Miss Kaye.

EMILIE. Yes?

NURSE. Arthur says he'll only speak to you. He had a knife and was threatening the others.

OLDER WILLIAM. I should go.

EMILIE. Where is he now?

NURSE. He says he'll only speak to you.

EMILIE. Has he still got the knife?

NURSE. No, we managed to get him to the ground.

EMILIE. Bring him in here.

NURSE. Here?

EMILIE. Yes.

NURSE *exits.*

OLDER WILLIAM. Is that safe?

EMILIE. He wouldn't hurt me.

OLDER WILLIAM. How can you be sure?

EMILIE. I know what I'm doing.

Have a safe journey, William.

*He holds out his hand. After a moment* EMILIE *takes it.*

OLDER WILLIAM. Look after yourself.

*He exits.*

*As he leaves,* NURSE *enters with* ARTHUR, *he's been in a fight.*

EMILIE. Hello Arthur.

(*To* NURSE.) You can leave, thank you.

NURSE *exits.*

What have you done to yourself?

*She approaches him and reaches towards his face. He flinches when she touches it.*

Who started it?

*No response.*

You told Nurse you'd only speak to me. So?

*Pause.*

That was my brother. That man leaving as you came in, that was my brother William. He's a famous biologist, do you know what that is?

ARTHUR *shrugs.*

He has a particular passion for corals, he's an expert, made contributions, discovered things. When he was a boy, no one thought he'd amount to anything, but I always knew he would.

When I was a girl, if I didn't do well in my lessons, I would be punished. Locked up in a room or the cellar on my own, sometimes for days at a time. I'd sob, I wanted to be good, I really did, but I came to the conclusion that goodness was impossible, or at least for me.

Is that how you feel?

*Pause.*

Goodness isn't impossible, Arthur.

ARTHUR. You don't know.

EMILIE. What don't I know?

Look at me.

*He looks at her.*

What don't I know?

ARTHUR. There's no good in me.

EMILIE. You feel hate. I can see it.

You feel hate so intense you can't keep still.

I've felt that.

ARTHUR. You?

EMILIE. I've felt so much hate I devoted my body and soul to
the Evil Spirit.

I've felt I could put an end to myself.

I've felt hatred towards everyone and a desire to make them
as wretched as me. Hell was in me.

Is that how you feel?

ARTHUR *looks at her.*

I see goodness in you, Arthur.

I was right about my brother, look at him now.

If there's goodness in me, there's goodness in you too,
I promise you that.

Now, will you let me stitch that eye?

ARTHUR *relents.*

*She tends to his face, very gently, with great kindness and
patience.*

CONSTANCE (*sixteen*) *approaches the cot where* SAVILLE *sleeps. She folds back the covers neatly and lifts him out of the cot.*

WILLIAM (*fifteen*) *appears.*

**www.nickhernbooks.co.uk**

facebook.com/nickhernbooks

twitter.com/nickhernbooks